PERSONAL INFORMATION

NAME

ADDRESS

HOME TELEPHONE   MOBILE

E-MAIL

BUSINESS ADDRESS

TELEPHONE

FAX

E-MAIL

WEBSITE

DOCTOR   TELEPHONE

BLOOD TYPE   RH   ALLERGIES

VACCINES   VALID UNTIL

VACCINES   VALID UNTIL

VACCINES   VALID UNTIL

IDENTITY CARD NO.   VALID UNTIL

PASSPORT   VALID UNTIL

ISSUED ON

VISA   VALID UNTIL

VISA   VALID UNTIL

DRIVER'S LICENSE   VALID UNTIL

CAR REGISTRATION NO.

MOTORCYCLE REGISTRATION NO.

BANK ACCOUNT NO.

CREDIT CARD   VALID UNTIL

MEDICAL INSURANCE COMPANY

TRAVEL INSURANCE

IN CASE OF ACCIDENT PLEASE NOTIFY

NAME

ADDRESS   TELEPHONE

PAULO COELHO

WISDOM

Diary
2011

RANDOM HOUSE MONDADORI

WISDOM

What kind of old age we have
depends on the manner in which we live.
We can choose to end up
like a ghost town or like a generous tree,
which continues to be important,
even when it can no longer stand.

CHRONICLE: REFLECTIONS ON OLD AGE

2011

JANUARY

S	M	T	W	T	F	S
						1
2	3	4	5	6	7	8
9	10	11	12	13	14	15
16	17	18	19	20	21	22
23	24	25	26	27	28	29
30	31					

1 New Year's Day
17 Martin Luther King Day

FEBRUARY

S	M	T	W	T	F	S
		1	2	3	4	5
6	7	8	9	10	11	12
13	14	15	16	17	18	19
20	21	22	23	24	25	26
27	28					

21 Presidents' Day

MARCH

S	M	T	W	T	F	S
		1	2	3	4	5
6	7	8	9	10	11	12
13	14	15	16	17	18	19
20	21	22	23	24	25	26
27	28	29	30	31		

APRIL

S	M	T	W	T	F	S
					1	2
3	4	5	6	7	8	9
10	11	12	13	14	15	16
17	18	19	20	21	22	23
24	25	26	27	28	29	30

22 Good Friday
24 Easter Sunday

MAY

S	M	T	W	T	F	S
1	2	3	4	5	6	7
8	9	10	11	12	13	14
15	16	17	18	19	20	21
22	23	24	25	26	27	28
29	30	31				

30 Memorial Day

JUNE

S	M	T	W	T	F	S
			1	2	3	4
5	6	7	8	9	10	11
12	13	14	15	16	17	18
19	20	21	22	23	24	25
26	27	28	29	30		

JULY

S	M	T	W	T	F	S
					1	2
3	4	5	6	7	8	9
10	11	12	13	14	15	16
17	18	19	20	21	22	23
24	25	26	27	28	29	30
31						

4 Independence Day

AUGUST

S	M	T	W	T	F	S
	1	2	3	4	5	6
7	8	9	10	11	12	13
14	15	16	17	18	19	20
21	22	23	24	25	26	27
28	29	30	31			

SEPTEMBER

S	M	T	W	T	F	S
				1	2	3
4	5	6	7	8	9	10
11	12	13	14	15	16	17
18	19	20	21	22	23	24
25	26	27	28	29	30	

5 Labor Day

OCTOBER

S	M	T	W	T	F	S
						1
2	3	4	5	6	7	8
9	10	11	12	13	14	15
16	17	18	19	20	21	22
23	24	25	26	27	28	29
30	31					

10 Columbus Day
31 Halloween

NOVEMBER

S	M	T	W	T	F	S
		1	2	3	4	5
6	7	8	9	10	11	12
13	14	15	16	17	18	19
20	21	22	23	24	25	26
27	28	29	30			

11 Veterans Day
24 Thanksgiving Day

DECEMBER

S	M	T	W	T	F	S
				1	2	3
4	5	6	7	8	9	10
11	12	13	14	15	16	17
18	19	20	21	22	23	24
25	26	27	28	29	30	31

25 Christmas Day

2012

JANUARY

S	M	T	W	T	F	S
1	2	3	4	5	6	7
8	9	10	11	12	13	14
15	16	17	18	19	20	21
22	23	24	25	26	27	28
29	30	31				

1 New Year's Day
16 Martin Luther King Day

FEBRUARY

S	M	T	W	T	F	S
			1	2	3	4
5	6	7	8	9	10	11
12	13	14	15	16	17	18
19	20	21	22	23	24	25
26	27	28	29			

20 Presidents' Day

MARCH

S	M	T	W	T	F	S
				1	2	3
4	5	6	7	8	9	10
11	12	13	14	15	16	17
18	19	20	21	22	23	24
25	26	27	28	29	30	31

APRIL

S	M	T	W	T	F	S
1	2	3	4	5	6	7
8	9	10	11	12	13	14
15	16	17	18	19	20	21
22	23	24	25	26	27	28
29	30					

6 Good Friday
8 Easter Sunday

MAY

S	M	T	W	T	F	S
		1	2	3	4	5
6	7	8	9	10	11	12
13	14	15	16	17	18	19
20	21	22	23	24	25	26
27	28	29	30	31		

28 Memorial Day

JUNE

S	M	T	W	T	F	S
					1	2
3	4	5	6	7	8	9
10	11	12	13	14	15	16
17	18	19	20	21	22	23
24	25	26	27	28	29	30

JULY

S	M	T	W	T	F	S
1	2	3	4	5	6	7
8	9	10	11	12	13	14
15	16	17	18	19	20	21
22	23	24	25	26	27	28
29	30	31				

4 Independence Day

AUGUST

S	M	T	W	T	F	S
			1	2	3	4
5	6	7	8	9	10	11
12	13	14	15	16	17	18
19	20	21	22	23	24	25
26	27	28	29	30	31	

SEPTEMBER

S	M	T	W	T	F	S
						1
2	3	4	5	6	7	8
9	10	11	12	13	14	15
16	17	18	19	20	21	22
23	24	25	26	27	28	29
30						

3 Labor Day

OCTOBER

S	M	T	W	T	F	S
	1	2	3	4	5	6
7	8	9	10	11	12	13
14	15	16	17	18	19	20
21	22	23	24	25	26	27
28	29	30	31			

8 Columbus Day
31 Halloween

NOVEMBER

S	M	T	W	T	F	S
				1	2	3
4	5	6	7	8	9	10
11	12	13	14	15	16	17
18	19	20	21	22	23	24
25	26	27	28	29	30	

6 Election Day
11 Veterans Day
12 Veterans Day (observed)
22 Thanksgiving Day

DECEMBER

S	M	T	W	T	F	S
						1
2	3	4	5	6	7	8
9	10	11	12	13	14	15
16	17	18	19	20	21	22
23	24	25	26	27	28	29
30	31					

25 Christmas Day

2011 YEAR PLANNER

JANUARY			FEBRUARY			MARCH		
S	1		T	1		T	1	
S	2		W	2	●	W	2	
M	3		T	3		T	3	
T	4	●	F	4		F	4	●
W	5		S	5		S	5	
T	6		S	6		S	6	
F	7		M	7		M	7	
S	8		T	8		T	8	
S	9		W	9		W	9	
M	10		T	10		T	10	
T	11		F	11	◗	F	11	
W	12	◗	S	12		S	12	◗
T	13		S	13		S	13	
F	14		M	14		M	14	
S	15		T	15		T	15	
S	16		W	16		W	16	
M	17		T	17		T	17	
T	18		F	18	○	F	18	
W	19	○	S	19		S	19	○
T	20		S	20		S	20	
F	21		M	21		M	21	
S	22		T	22		T	22	
S	23		W	23		W	23	
M	24		T	24	◖	T	24	
T	25		F	25		F	25	
W	26	◖	S	26		S	26	◖
T	27		S	27		S	27	
F	28		M	28		M	28	
S	29					T	29	
S	30					W	30	
M	31					T	31	

F	1
S	2
S	**3** ●
M	4
T	5
W	6
T	7
F	8
S	9
S	**10**
M	11 ◐
T	12
W	13
T	14
F	15
S	16
S	**17** ○
M	18
T	19
W	20
T	21
F	22
S	23
S	**24** ◑
M	25
T	26
W	27
T	28
F	29
S	30

S	**1**
M	2
T	3 ●
W	4
T	5
F	6
S	7
S	**8**
M	9
T	10 ◐
W	11
T	12
F	13
S	14
S	**15**
M	16
T	17 ○
W	18
T	19
F	20
S	21
S	**22**
M	23
T	24 ◑
W	25
T	26
F	27
S	28
S	**29**
M	30
T	31

W	1 ●
T	2
F	3
S	4
S	**5**
M	6
T	7
W	8 ◐
T	9
F	10
S	11
S	**12**
M	13
T	14
W	15 ○
T	16
F	17
S	18
S	**19**
M	20
T	21
W	22
T	23 ◑
F	24
S	25
S	**26**
M	27
T	28
W	29
T	30

2011 YEAR PLANNER

JULY				AUGUST				SEPTEMBER		
F	1	●	M	1		T	1	
S	2		T	2		F	2	
S	**3**		W	3		S	3	
M	4		T	4		S	**4**	◗
T	5		F	5		M	5	
W	6		S	6	◖	T	6	
T	7		S	**7**		W	7	
F	8	◗	M	8		T	8	
S	9		T	9		F	9	
S	**10**		W	10		S	10	
M	11		T	11		S	**11**	
T	12		F	12		M	12	○
W	13		S	13	○	T	13	
T	14		S	**14**		W	14	
F	15	○	M	15		T	15	
S	16		T	16		F	16	
S	**17**		W	17		S	17	
M	18		T	18		S	**18**	
T	19		F	19		M	19	
W	20		S	20		T	20	◖
T	21		S	**21**	◗	W	21	
F	22		M	22		T	22	
S	23	◖	T	23		F	23	
S	**24**		W	24		S	24	
M	25		T	25		S	**25**	
T	26		F	26		M	26	
W	27		S	27		T	27	●
T	28		S	**28**	●	W	28	
F	29		M	29		T	29	
S	30	●	T	30		F	30	
S	**31**		W	31				

S	1	
S	**2**	
M	3	◑
T	4	
W	5	
T	6	
F	7	
S	8	
S	**9**	
M	10	
T	11	○
W	12	
T	13	
F	14	
S	15	
S	**16**	
M	17	
T	18	
W	19	◐
T	20	
F	21	
S	22	
S	**23**	
M	24	
T	25	
W	26	●
T	27	
F	28	
S	29	
S	**30**	
M	31	

T	1	
W	2	◐
T	3	
F	4	
S	5	
S	**6**	
M	7	
T	8	
W	9	
T	10	○
F	11	
S	12	
S	**13**	
M	14	
T	15	
W	16	
T	17	
F	18	◐
S	19	
S	**20**	
M	21	
T	22	
W	23	
T	24	
F	25	●
S	26	
S	**27**	
M	28	
T	29	
W	30	

T	1	
F	2	◐
S	3	
S	**4**	
M	5	
T	6	
W	7	
T	8	
F	9	
S	10	○
S	**11**	
M	12	
T	13	
W	14	
T	15	
F	16	
S	17	◐
S	**18**	
M	19	
T	20	
W	21	
T	22	
F	23	
S	24	●
S	**25**	
M	26	
T	27	
W	28	
T	29	
F	30	
S	31	

The ceremony is an adoration
of all that is beautiful and simple.
It is focused entirely upon the attempt to achieve
Perfection through the imperfect gestures of daily life.
If having a cup of tea with someone
can transport us to God, then we should remain alert
for the dozens of other opportunities life offers us.

NOTES FROM MY NON-EXISTENT DIARY

JANUARY *Blessing*

1 Saturday

2 Sunday

The closer we grow to God through faith, the simpler He becomes.
And the simpler He becomes, the stronger is His presence.

BY THE RIVER PIEDRA I SAT DOWN AND WEPT

3 | Monday

4 | Tuesday

What are the three conditions you need
to meet before you can talk with the angels?
Break an agreement. Accept forgiveness. And place a bet.

THE VALKYRIES

5 Wednesday

6 Thursday

7 Friday

8 Saturday

9 Sunday

Quite by accident he had begun
to discover the presence of God in everything he did.
Every table he made, every chair he carved,
helped him to realize that life is sacred and that small things
are important in the transformation of the Universe.
His trade became his real apprenticeship;
nothing he did was pointless and each moment
carried within it eternity and the whole of Creation.

THE FIFTH MOUNTAIN

10 Monday

11 Tuesday

Everything is permitted,
apart from interrupting a display of Love.
When that happens, the would-be destroyer
is forced to start rebuilding all over again.

THE PILGRIMAGE

12 Wednesday

13 Thursday

14 Friday

15 Saturday

16 Sunday

There's no need to enter a seminary, to fast,
abstain or take a vow of chastity in order to lead a spiritual life.
All you have to do is keep faith and accept God.
From then on, each of us becomes a part of His Path,
we become the vehicle for His miracles.

BY THE RIVER PIEDRA I SAT DOWN AND WEPT

17 Monday

18 Tuesday

It doesn't matter what we do,
each of us is playing a central role in the History of the World.

THE ALCHEMIST

19 Wednesday

20 Thursday

21 Friday

22 Saturday

23 Sunday

There are moments when you simply have to accept
the mystery and understand that each person has his or her own gift.
Some have the gift of healing, others of wisdom,
still others can converse with the spirits.
It is through the sum of these gifts that God can reveal His glory,
using humankind as his instruments.

THE VALKYRIES

24 Monday

25 Tuesday

The angel is always protecting us, and that is a divine gift,
there is no need to invoke him.
The face of your angel is always visible
when you see the world through the eyes of beauty.

THE PILGRIMAGE

2 6 Wednesday

2 7 Thursday

28 Friday

29 Saturday

30 Sunday

We do not believe that God made the Universe.
We believe that God is the Universe,
and we are contained in Him, and He in us.

THE WITCH OF PORTOBELLO

Week 5

31 Monday

Sooner or later we must overcome our fears,
because the spiritual path
is traveled through the daily experience of love.

BY THE RIVER PIEDRA I SAT DOWN AND WEPT

FEBRUARY *Reflection*

The future is knocking at our door,
and every idea—except those that are mere prejudices
will have a chance of appearing and being valued by others.
Useless ideas will vanish.
We are not the judges of our neighbor's dreams
and have no right to censure them.
In order to have faith in our path,
we do not need to prove that someone else's path is wrong.
Anyone who behaves like this clearly
has no confidence in the steps he himself is taking.

MAKTUB

1 Tuesday

Each human being carries within him something far more important
than his own self, namely, his particular Gift.
For God placed in the hands of each and every one of us a Gift,
the instrument He used to reveal Himself to the world and to help humanity

BRIDA

2 Wednesday

3 Thursday

4 Friday

5 Saturday

6 Sunday

This is what Alchemists do.
They show that, when we seek to be better than we are,
everything around us becomes better too.

THE ALCHEMIST

7 Monday

8 Tuesday

Fear makes us ashamed of showing our love.

BY THE RIVER PIEDRA I SAT DOWN AND WEPT

9 Wednesday

10 Thursday

11 Friday

12 Saturday

13   Sunday

The challenge will not wait. Life does not look back.
A week is more than enough time for us
to decide whether or not to accept our destiny.

THE DEVIL AND MISS PRYM

14 Monday

15 Tuesday

People have been trying to understand the Universe
through love ever since the beginning of time.

BRIDA

16 Wednesday

17 Thursday

18 Friday

19 Saturday

20 Sunday

An encounter with the superior energy is open to anyone,
but remains far from those who shift responsibility onto others.

THE WITCH OF PORTOBELLO

21 Monday

22 Tuesday

God is in life and life is in God.
If we can penetrate the sacred harmony of everyday life,
we will be on the right path
because our daily tasks are also our divine tasks.

CHRONICLE: DIALOGUES WITH THE MASTER

2 3 Wednesday

2 4 Thursday

25 Friday

26 Saturday

27 Sunday

A warrior can distinguish what is transient from what will endure.

MANUAL OF THE WARRIOR OF LIGHT

2 8 Monday

When we accept the inevitable encounter with other sources,
we will, in the end, understand that this makes us stronger,
we will flow around obstacles
and fill in depressions more quickly and more easily.

CHRONICLE: UNDERSTANDING THE RIVER

MARCH *Learning*

If we love what we do,
we can transform slavery into liberty.
If we cannot,
then it would be best to stop now.

CHRONICLE: CREATIVE SOLUTIONS

1 Tuesday

I learned that the world has a Soul
and anyone capable of understanding that Soul
can understand the language of all things.

THE ALCHEMIST

2 Wednesday

3 Thursday

4 Friday

5 Saturday

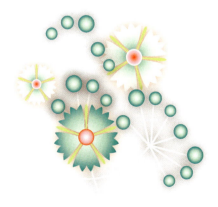

6 Sunday

Free will demands immense responsibility;
it's hard work and brings with it anguish and suffering.

THE WITCH OF PORTOBELLO

7 Monday

8 Tuesday

He needed wings too.
They reveal to us the endless horizons of the imagination,
they carry us to our dreams and to distant places.
It is our wings that allow us to know
the roots of our fellow men and to learn from them.

THE WINNER STANDS ALONE

9 Wednesday

10 Thursday

11 Friday

12 Saturday

13 Sunday

The gates of Paradise are open to those who are determined to enter.
The world lies in the hands of those who
have the courage to dream and to live out their dreams.

THE VALKYRIES

MARCH

Week 11

14 Monday

15 Tuesday

The person who succeeds in being what he or she
dreamed of being for ten minutes each day is making great progress.

CHRONICLE: DIALOGUES WITH THE MASTER

16 Wednesday

17 Thursday

18 Friday

19 Saturday

20 Sunday

The soul loves all things beautiful and deep.

THE WINNER STANDS ALONE

21 | Monday

22 | Tuesday

People have been searching for their Soulmate since time began,
by looking into another person's eyes in search of that special light, desire.

BRIDA

2 3 Wednesday

2 4 Thursday

25 Friday

26 Saturday

Week 12

2 7 Sunday

The universe only makes sense
when we have someone to share our feelings with.

E L E V E N   M I N U T E S

28 Monday

29 Tuesday

The energy of the Earth needs to be constantly renewed.
Body and soul need new paths
so that they can come together in harmony.

CHRONICLE: AN END TO PRECONCEPTIONS

30 Wednesday

31 Thursday

APRIL *Certainty*

There are moments
when you still need to take risks,
to do something crazy.

BY THE RIVER PIEDRA I SAT DOWN AND WEPT

1 Friday

2 Saturday

3 Sunday

She knew that the best way to immerse herself in God was through love.

BRIDA

ιday

5 Tuesday

Whoever you are or whatever you have done,
when you really want something,
it's because that desire was born in the soul of the Universe.
That is your mission on Earth.

THE ALCHEMIST

6 Wednesday

7 Thursday

8 Friday

9 Saturday

10   Sunday

The prime virtue in someone seeking the spiritual path is courage.

THE VALKYRIES

11 Monday

12 Tuesday

There's no such thing as a "one and only chance";
life always gives you another opportunity.

THE WINNER STANDS ALONE

13 Wednesday

14 Thursday

15 Friday

16 Saturday

17 Sunday

I think that when we seek love with courage,
love reveals itself and we attract more love.

BY THE RIVER PIEDRA I SAT DOWN AND WEPT

18 Monday

19 Tuesday

As long as there were people who knew that,
in God's eyes, all of man's wisdom was madness,
the world would continue along the path of light.

BRIDA

20 Wednesday

21 Thursday

22 Friday

23 Saturday

2 4 Sunday

Love is not to be found in someone else, but in ourselves;
we simply awaken it.
But in order to do that, we need the other person.

ELEVEN MINUTES

25 Monday

26 Tuesday

No one can lie or hide anything
when someone looks them straight in the eye.

BY THE RIVER PIEDRA I SAT DOWN AND WEPT

2 7 Wednesday

2 8 Thursday

29 Friday

30 Saturday

Warriors of light are not always quite sure what they are doing here.
They spend many sleepless nights,
believing that their lives have no meaning.
That is why they are warriors of light.
Because they make mistakes. Because they ask themselves questions.
Because they are looking for a reason—and are sure to find it.

CHRONICLE – THE WARRIOR OF LIGHT AND HIS WORLD

The simple things are the most extraordinary,
and only the wise can see them.

THE ALCHEMIST

MAY *Creativity*

1 Sunday

At the first sign of indifference or lack of enthusiasm, take note!
The only preventive against this disease
is the realization that the soul suffers, suffers greatly,
when we force it to live superficially.
The soul loves all things beautiful and deep.

THE WINNER STANDS ALONE

2 Monday

3 Tuesday

In war, the key to victory is the ability to surprise one's opponent.

MANUAL OF THE WARRIOR OF LIGHT

4 Wednesday

5 Thursday

6 Friday

7 Saturday

8 Sunday

On the path of life,
we will always find problems that are hard to resolve.
That is when you need to
let your Creative Imagination take over.

THE PILGRIMAGE

9 Monday

10 Tuesday

The warrior realizes that there are difficulties
he had not reckoned with.
If he waits for the ideal moment, he will never set off,
and people are always telling him
that what he is about to do is utter madness.
The warrior uses that touch of madness.
For—in love as in war—it is impossible to foresee everything.

CHRONICLE – THE WARRIOR OF LIGHT AND HIS WORLD

11 Wednesday

12 Thursday

13 Friday

14 Saturday

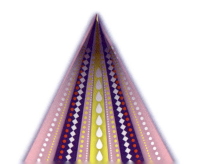

15 Sunday

Train your eyes: they were made to see more than you think.

THE WITCH OF PORTOBELLO

MAY

Week 20

16 Monday

17 Tuesday

A warrior takes every opportunity to teach himself.

MANUAL OF THE WARRIOR OF LIGHT

18 Wednesday

19 Thursday

20 Friday

21 Saturday

22 Sunday

The really important meetings
are planned by our souls long before our bodies meet.

ELEVEN MINUTES

23 Monday

24 Tuesday

Let go of the idea that the path will lead you to your goal.
The truth is that with each step we take, we arrive.

THE WITCH OF PORTOBELLO

2 5 Wednesday

2 6 Thursday

27 Friday

28 Saturday

2 9 Sunday

All energy and all knowledge
come from the same unknown source,
which we usually call God.

THE ZAHIR

30 Monday

31 Tuesday

It is precisely the possibility of realizing a dream
that makes life interesting.

THE ALCHEMIST

JUNE *Autonomy*

A responsible warrior is not someone
who takes the weight of the world on his shoulders,
but someone who has learned
to deal with the challenges of the moment.

CHRONICLE – RESPONSIBILITY AND RISK

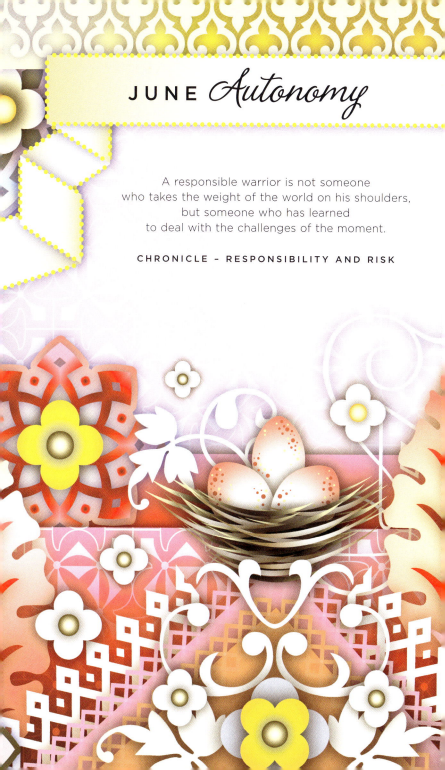

We don't always notice the immense Joy
that exists in the heart of someone engaged in the struggle,
because they don't care about victory or defeat;
what matters is fighting the Good Fight.

THE PILGRIMAGE

1 Wednesday

2 Thursday

3 Friday

4 Saturday

5 Sunday

The path begins at a crossroads.
There you can stop and think about which direction to take.
But don't think for too long or you'll never set off.

CHRONICLE – MANUAL FOR PRESERVING PATHS

6 Monday

7 Tuesday

Play your part and don't worry about what others do.
Believe that God also speaks to them,
and that they are as engaged as you are in discovering the meaning of life.

BRIDA

8 Wednesday

9 Thursday

10 Friday

11 Saturday

12 | Sunday

You have found your path.
Few people have the courage to do so.
They prefer to follow a path that is not their own.

BRIDA

13 Monday

14 Tuesday

Faith parries all blows. Faith transforms poison into crystalline water.

CHRONICLE – THE WARRIOR OF LIGHT AND HIS WORLD

15 Wednesday

16 Thursday

17 Friday

18 Saturday

19 Sunday

Sometimes it's impossible to stop the river of life.

THE ALCHEMIST

20 Monday

21 Tuesday

I would like to believe that I will see this new year as if it were
the first time that 365 days had passed before my eyes,
that I will see the people around me with surprise and amazement,
glad to discover that they are by my side sharing that
much-talked-about, but little-understood thing called "love."

CHRONICLE – AS IF FOR THE FIRST TIME

22 Wednesday

23 Thursday

24 Friday

25 Saturday

2 6 Sunday

I would like not to control my heart.
If I could give my heart away, even if only for a weekend,
this rain falling on my face would have another taste entirely.

BY THE RIVER PIEDRA I SAT DOWN AND WEPT

27 Monday

28 Tuesday

Let us allow our angel to speak in the way he usually does,
whenever he feels it's necessary.
Advice is only theory; living is something else altogether.

CHRONICLE – DIALOGUES WITH THE MASTER

29 Wednesday

30 Thursday

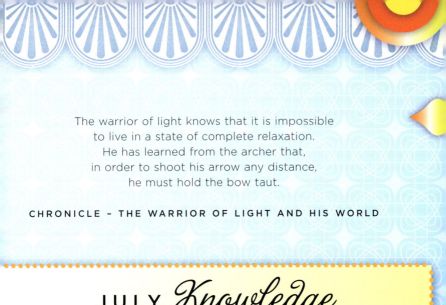

The warrior of light knows that it is impossible
to live in a state of complete relaxation.
He has learned from the archer that,
in order to shoot his arrow any distance,
he must hold the bow taut.

CHRONICLE – THE WARRIOR OF LIGHT AND HIS WORLD

JULY *Knowledge*

2 Saturday

3 Sunday

A warrior of light knows that in the silence of his heart
he will hear an order that will guide him.

MANUAL OF THE WARRIOR OF LIGHT

4 Monday

5 Tuesday

I carry with me the marks and scars of battles—
they are the witnesses of what I have suffered
and the rewards of what I have conquered.
These are the beloved marks and scars
that will open the gates of Paradise to me.

CHRONICLE – THE IMPORTANCE OF SAYING "NO"

6 Wednesday

7 Thursday

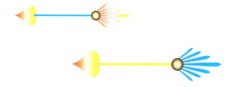

8 Friday

9 Saturday

10 Sunday

A day will come when those knocking at the door will see it open;
those who ask will receive; those who weep will be consoled.

THE VALKYRIES

11 Monday

12 Tuesday

The true path of knowledge has three identifying features.
First, it must include Agape;
second, it must have some practical application in life,
otherwise knowledge will become a useless thing
and will rust like a sword that is never unsheathed.
And, finally, it must be a path that can be followed by anyone.

THE PILGRIMAGE

13 Wednesday

14 Thursday

15 Friday

16 Saturday

17 Sunday

Our souls have a kind of meteorological service,
and to avoid a great deal of personal and professional wear and tear,
all you have to do is not to underestimate
the importance of apparently inoffensive things.

CHRONICLE – CRISES AND THEIR TRAPS

18 Monday

19 Tuesday

When you want something,
the whole Universe conspires in your favor.

THE ALCHEMIST

20 Wednesday

21 Thursday

22 Friday

23 Saturday

2 4 Sunday

The greatness of God is evident in any task,
but especially in those tasks carried out with love.

THE FIFTH MOUNTAIN

LY

y

26 Tuesday

Pain was no longer a cause of suffering,
but a source of pleasure because they were
redeeming humanity from its sins.
Pain became joy, the meaning of life, pleasure.

ELEVEN MINUTES

27 Wednesday

28 Thursday

29 Friday

30 Saturday

31 Sunday

Human beings are all the same.
If you try to hold on to them in some way,
they'll escape,
but if you're gentle with them,
they'll stay by your side forever.

CHRONICLE – CONVERSATIONS WITH CHILDREN

AUGUST *Good Sense*

Do not be ashamed
to make a temporary withdrawal from the field
if you see that your enemy is stronger than you;
it is not winning or losing a single battle that matters,
but how the war ends.

MANUAL OF THE WARRIOR OF LIGHT

1 Monday

2 Tuesday

The Universe is made up of a language
that everyone understands,
but which they have forgotten.
I am looking for that Universal Language.

THE ALCHEMIST

3 Wednesday

4 Thursday

5 Friday

6 Saturday

7 Sunday

We are all masters of our own destiny.
We can so easily make the same mistakes over and over.
We can so easily flee from everything that we desire
and which life so generously places before us.

BRIDA

AUGUST

--

8 Monday

9 Tuesday

A warrior always returns to the fray.
He never does so out of stubbornness,
but because he has noticed a change in the weather.

MANUAL OF THE WARRIOR OF LIGHT

10 Wednesday

11 Thursday

12 Friday

13 Saturday

14 Sunday

A child can teach an adult three things:
to be happy for no reason, to be always busy with something,
and to know how to demand, with all his might, what he wants.

THE FIFTH MOUNTAIN

15 Monday

16 Tuesday

Work reflects the amount of energy you put into it.
There is no such thing as a bad job.
If you're not happy, then take a risk and change everything
so that you can devote yourself to what you love.
Better to be happy on a small salary
than unhappy because you're afraid to change.

CHRONICLE – RESPECTING WORK

17 Wednesday

18 Thursday

19 Friday

20 Saturday

21 Sunday

Life is too short, or too long,
for me to allow myself the luxury of living it so badly.

ELEVEN MINUTES

2 2 Monday

2 3 Tuesday

If you're looking for new and different horizons,
observe the other people around you,
but never try to act exactly as they do,
because life's paths are many and various.

CHRONICLE – REFLECTING SOMEONE ELSE'S LIGHT

24 Wednesday

25 Thursday

26 Friday

27 Saturday

A

2 8 Sunday

All the great men and women of the world
were people who rather than saying "Yes,"
said a very loud "No"
to everything that went against
their ideal of goodness and growth.

CHRONICLE – THE IMPORTANCE OF SAYING "NO"

29 Monday

30 Tuesday

Anyone who fails to recognize problems
leaves the door open for tragedies to rush in.

MANUAL OF THE WARRIOR OF LIGHT

31 Wednesday

SEPTEMBER *Respectability*

In order to forget the rules,
you must know them and respect them,
because the path is more important
than whatever made you set off along it.

THE WITCH OF PORTOBELLO

Week 35

SEPTEMBER

---

1 Thursday

Follow your dreams, because only someone
who is not ashamed of himself
can make manifest the glory of God.

THE VALKYRIES

2 Friday

3 Saturday

Honor your path.
It was your choice and your decision,
and if you respect the ground on which you walk,
the ground will respect your feet.
Always do your best to preserve and maintain the path
and it will do the same for you.

CHRONICLE – MANUAL FOR PRESERVING PATHS

4 Sunday

5 Monday

6 Tuesday

7 Wednesday

8 Thursday

Desire is not what you see, but what you imagine.

ELEVEN MINUTES

9 Friday

10 Saturday

Discover your own light,
if you don't, you will spend the rest of your life
being nothing but the pale reflection
of someone else's light.

CHRONICLE – REFLECTING SOMEONE ELSE'S LIGHT

11 Sunday

12 Monday

13 Tuesday

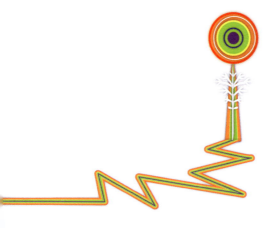

14 Wednesday

15 Thursday

A sense of gratitude is important;
no one gets very far if he forgets
those who were with him in his hour of need.
Not that you have to be constantly
thinking about who helped or was helped.
God has His eyes fixed on his sons and daughters
and rewards only those who behave in accordance with
the blessings that were bestowed on them.

THE WINNER STANDS ALONE

16 Friday

17 Saturday

A warrior of light dances with his companions,
but does not place the responsibility for his actions on anyone else.

MANUAL OF THE WARRIOR OF LIGHT

18 Sunday

19 Monday

20 Tuesday

21 Wednesday

22 Thursday

We have all spent many days or even whole weeks
without receiving a single affectionate word or gesture from another person.
At such times, we must put more wood on the fire
and try to light up the dark room our life has become.
If we are capable of love, we are also capable of receiving love;
it's only a matter of time.

CHRONICLE – KINDNESS

2 3 Friday

2 4 Saturday

The man who defends his friends
is never overwhelmed by the storms of life;
he is strong enough to come through
difficulties and to carry on.

MANUAL OF THE WARRIOR OF LIGHT

2 5　Sunday

2 6 Monday

2 7 Tuesday

2 8 Wednesday

2 9 Thursday

There's nothing wrong with doing simple things.

THE WITCH OF PORTOBELLO

30 Friday

Lessons always arrive when you are ready,
and if you can read the signs,
you will learn everything you need to know
in order to take the next step.

THE ZAHIR

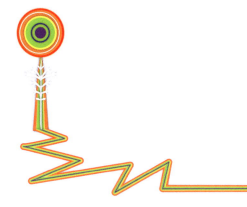

Freedom was feeling what his heart desired,
regardless of what other people thought.

THE FIFTH MOUNTAIN

OCTOBER *Justice*

1 Saturday

The act of forgiveness does not mean
that a warrior must accept everything;
he cannot bow his head, for if he did
he would lose sight of the horizon of his dreams.

CHRONICLE – ACCEPTING PARADOXES

2 | Sunday

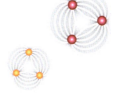

3 Monday

4 Tuesday

5 Wednesday

6 Thursday

There are two kinds of idiot—those who take no action
because they have received a threat,
and those who think they are taking action
because they have issued a threat.

THE DEVIL AND MISS PRYM

7 Friday

8 Saturday

The Universe does not judge;
it conspires in favor of what we want.
That is why the warrior has the courage
to look into the dark places of his soul
and try to illuminate them
with the light of forgiveness.

CHRONICLE – THE WARRIOR OF LIGHT AND THE NEW YEAR

9 Sunday

10 Monday

11 Tuesday

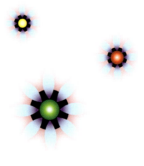

12 Wednesday

13 Thursday

"It was a mistake that set the world in motion," said the Teacher.
"Never be afraid of making a mistake."

BRIDA

14 Friday

15 Saturday

The warrior says to himself:
"I fought for something and did not succeed. I lost the first battle."
These words give him renewed strength.
He knows that no one wins all the time,
but that the brave always win in the end.

CHRONICLE – THE DECISIONS OF THE WARRIOR

16 Sunday

17 Monday

18 Tuesday

19 Wednesday

20 Thursday

Avoid routine and seek out the extraordinary.
That small thing, however tiny, could open the door
to a great adventure, both human and spiritual.

CHRONICLE – MYSTERIES

21 Friday

22 Saturday

It is good that you have learned that everything in life has a price.
That is what the warriors of light try to teach.

THE ALCHEMIST

2 3   Sunday

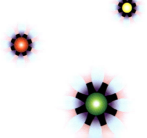

24 Monday

25 Tuesday

2 6 Wednesday

2 7 Thursday

In the worst of all my crises, my friends were there for me.
Ever since then, the first thing I do is to ask for help.

CHRONICLE – CRISES AND THEIR TRAPS

2 8 Friday

_____

_____

_____

_____

_____

_____

_____

_____

_____

_____

2 9 Saturday

_____

_____

_____

_____

_____

_____

_____

_____

_____

_____

Many sail the current of the inevitable and are shipwrecked;
others are swept away to places to which they were not intended to go.
But you have faced the voyage with dignity,
you were able to control your boat and transform pain into action.

THE FIFTH MOUNTAIN

Week 43

30 Sunday

31 | Monday

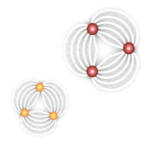

Our human condition makes us tend to share only the best of ourselves,
because we are always searching for love and approval.

THE ZAHIR

NOVEMBER *Understanding*

If things and events always went the way we wanted,
we would have nothing to talk about.
When faced by unpleasant situations that we cannot avoid, just relax.
The Universe continues to work for us in secret.

CHRONICLE – LIFE SITUATIONS

1 Tuesday

When you want something with all your heart,
you are closer to the Soul of the World,
which is always a positive force.

THE ALCHEMIST

2 Wednesday

3 Thursday

4 Friday

5 Saturday

6 | Sunday

Know that victories and defeats form part of everyone's life—
everyone, that is, except cowards, because they neither lose nor win.

THE DEVIL AND MISS PRYM

7 Monday

8 Tuesday

The two main mistakes in any strategy
are acting too soon or letting an opportunity slip.

CHRONICLE – ACCEPTING CHALLENGES

9 Wednesday

10 Thursday

11 Friday

12 Saturday

13 Sunday

What does learning mean:
accumulating knowledge or transforming your life?

THE WITCH OF PORTOBELLO

14 Monday

---

15 Tuesday

We lose our Enthusiasm because of the small,
but necessary defeats we suffer during the Good Fight.
And since we do not know that Enthusiasm is a major force
intent on the final victory, we let it slip through our fingers,
not realizing that we are also letting slip the real meaning of our lives.

THE PILGRIMAGE

16 Wednesday

17 Thursday

18 Friday

19 Saturday

20 Sunday

Don't forget that everything is one.
Don't forget the language of signs.
And, above all, don't forget to follow
your Personal Legend through to the end.

THE ALCHEMIST

21 Monday

22 Tuesday

I hope that you will behave
like other men given a second chance;
don't make the same mistake again.
Never forget the reason for your life.

THE FIFTH MOUNTAIN

2 3 Wednesday

2 4 Thursday

25 Friday

26 Saturday

2 7 Sunday

The true sage is delighted with his path,
but he is always aware of the traps that might lie ahead.

CHRONICLE – EDUCATING OURSELVES TO WIN

2 8 Monday

2 9 Tuesday

Life is in constant evolution on every level,
be it social, political or spiritual.
In order for people to evolve, they must change.

CHRONICLE – BOREDOM

30 Wednesday

Those who plant endure storms and all
the many vicissitudes of the seasons, and they rarely rest.
But, unlike a building, a garden never stops growing.
And while it requires the gardener's constant attention,
it also allows life for the gardener to be a great adventure.
Gardeners always recognize each other,
because they know that in the history of each plant
lies the growth of the whole World.

BRIDA

1 Thursday

Silence does not always mean consent—
usually all it means is that people
are incapable of coming up with an immediate response.

THE DEVIL AND MISS PRYM

2 Friday

3 Saturday

For the warrior, there is no "better" or "worse":
everyone has the necessary gifts for his particular path.

MANUAL OF THE WARRIOR OF LIGHT

4 Sunday

5 Monday

6 Tuesday

7 Wednesday

8 Thursday

It is very important to pay attention to the road.
It is the road that teaches us the best way to get there,
and the road enriches us as we walk its length.

THE PILGRIMAGE

9 Friday

10 Saturday

The human spirit feeds on mysteries and cannot live eternally
protected by a glass dome that guarantees
constant security and the achievement of our every goal.

CHRONICLE – MYSTERIES

11 Sunday

12 Monday

13 Tuesday

14 Wednesday

15 Thursday

If I can decipher that language without words,
I will be able to decipher the world.

THE ALCHEMIST

16 Friday

17 Saturday

Victory might give me confidence,
but it mustn't become a weight to be carried.

18 Sunday

19 Monday

20 Tuesday

21 Wednesday

22 Thursday

There is no greater pleasure
than that of initiating someone into an unknown world,
of taking someone's virginity—
the virginity not of their body, but of their soul.

ELEVEN MINUTES

DECEMBER

23 Friday

24 Saturday

Happiness cannot last.
It is always made up of moments,
so we can never just lie back on a mattress
and contemplate the world.

CHRONICLE – I'M NOT HAPPY

25 Sunday

26 Monday

27 Tuesday

28 Wednesday

29 Thursday

We must not forget that, in life,
things do not always turn out as we would like.
There are moments, for example,
when we seek something that is not meant for us.

CHRONICLE – LIFE SITUATIONS

30 Friday

31 Saturday

The angels are visible to those who accept
the light and break the pact with darkness.

THE VALKYRIES

Original title: *Sabedoria 2011*

Copyright © by Paulo Coelho and Forlagshuset Bazar AS, 2010
www.paulocoelhoblog.com

Published by agreement with
Sant Jordi Asociados Agencia Literaria, S.L.U, Barcelona (Spain)
www.santjordi-asociados.com

© 2010, English Language Rights for the USA
Random House Mondadori, S.A. de C. V.
Av. Homero núm. 544, col. Chapultepec Morales,
Delegación Miguel Hidalgo, 11570, México, D. F.

www.rhmx.com.mx

ISBN: 978-030-739-342-5

Edition by Marcia Botelho
Translation by: © Ana Belén Costas, Alfonso Indecona,
Montserrat Mira, Hinda Katia Schumer,
M. Dolors Ventós
Illustrations: Catalina Estrada at Folioart.co.uk, www.catalinaestrada.com

Photography: © Paul Macleod
Design: Lene Stangebye Geving

Printed and bound by TBB Slovakia, 2010